LEVEL
3

Walt Disney

Barbara Kramer

NATIONAL
GEOGRAPHIC

Washington, D.C.

To my sisters, Kathy, Marilyn, and Susan —B.K.

Library of Congress Cataloging-in-Publication Data
Names: Kramer, Barbara, author.
Title: National Geographic reader. Walt Disney / Barbara Kramer.
Description: Washington, DC : National Geographic Children's Books, 2017. | Series: National Geographic reader | Includes index. | Audience: Ages 6–9. | Audience: K to Grade 3.
Identifiers: LCCN 2017010736| ISBN 9781426326738 (paperback) | ISBN 9781426326745 (hardcover)
Subjects: LCSH: Disney, Walt, 1901-1966--Juvenile literature. | Animators--United States--Biography --Juvenile literature. | BISAC: JUVENILE NON-FICTION / Readers / Beginner. | JUVENILE NON-FICTION / Biography & Autobiography / General. | JUVENILE NONFICTION / People & Places / United States / General.
Classification: LCC NC1766.U52 D54515 2017 | DDC 741.58092 [B] --dc23
LC record available at https://lccn.loc.gov/2017010736

The author and publisher gratefully acknowledge the expert content review of this book by Dan Viets, Walt Disney historian and lecturer, and coauthor of *Walt Disney's Missouri: The Roots of a Creative Genius*, and the literacy review of this book by Mariam Jean Dreher, professor of reading education, University of Maryland, College Park.

Photo Credits

AL=Alamy Stock Photo; GI=Getty Images; LOC=Library of Congress Prints and Photographs Division; SS=Shutterstock

COVER: (background), RSBPhoto1/AL; (RT), HO Images/AL; INTERIOR: (throughout), corund/SS; 1, Alfred Eisenstaedt/GI; 3, Gene Lester/GI; 4 (LE), A.F. ARCHIVE/AL; 4 (CTR), Everett Collection/AL; 4 (UP), urbanbuzz/AL; 4 (RT), James Clews/AL; 5, Hulton Archive/GI; 6 (UP), Hulton Archive/GI; 6 (CTR), Bettmann/GI; 7 (UP), Bettmann/GI; 7 (LO), Buddy Mays/AL; 8, Hulton Archive/GI; 9 (UP), Apic/GI; 9 (LO), Iakov Filimonov/SS; 10, Walt Disney Hometown Museum; 11 (UP), Eric Farrelly/AL; 11 (LO), Apic/GI; 12, ClassicStock/AL; 13, Chicago History Museum/GI; 14 (CTR), Olivier Le Queinec/Dreamstime; 14 (LO), Chicago History Museum/GI; 15 (UP), Screenprod/AL; 15 (CTR), Richard Thornton/SS; 15 (LO), Bettmann/GI; 16, NG Maps; 17, Popperfoto/GI; 18, Thank You Walt Disney; 19 (UP), © Can Stock Photo/HomoErectus; 19 (LO), Alfred Eisenstaedt/GI; 20-21 (LO), Mitch Diamond/GI; 21 (CTR), Alfred Eisenstaedt/GI; 22 (UP), Hulton Archive/GI; 23 (UP), Bettmann/GI; 23 (LO), Ullstein Bild/GI; 24, Everett Collection, Inc./AL; 25, Ewing Galloway/Bridgeman Images; 26 (LO), Ullstein Bild/GI; 26 (CTR), Ullstein Bild/GI; 27 (UP), Ronald Grant Archive/AL; 28, Everett Collection, Inc./AL; 29, NBC/GI; 30 (UP), HeikeKampe/GI; 30 (CTR), Gene Lester/GI; 30 (LO), Hulton Archive/GI; 31 (UP), Bettmann/GI; 31 (CTR), Bettmann/GI; 31 (LO), Gene Lester/GI; 33, Earl Theisen Collection/GI; 34, Pictorial Press/AL; 35, Walt Disney Pictures/Ronald Grant Archive/AL; 36, AF Archive/AL; 37, ABC Photo Archives/GI; 38, Earl Theisen Collection/GI; 39 (CTR), Ullstein Bild/GI; 39 (UP), Carol M. Highsmith/LOC; 40-41 (LO), Julia-art/SS; 40 (CTR), AF Archive/AL; 41 (UP), dpa/ullstein bild/The Image Works; 42-43 (LO), Julia-art/SS; 42 (CTR), tim gartside usa america/AL; 43 (CTR), Bloomberg/GI; 44 (UP), Paul Stringer/SS; 44 (CTR), Chicago History Museum/GI; 44 (LO), Thank You Walt Disney; 45 (UP), Ronald Grant Archive/AL; 45 (CTR RT), Earl Theisen Collection/GI; 45 (CTR LE), imageBROKER/AL; 45 (LO), Carol M. Highsmith/LOC; 46 (UP), © Can Stock Photo/HomoErectus; 46 (CTR LE), Hulton Archive/GI; 46 (CTR RT), AF Archive/AL; 46 (LO LE), Ascent XMedia/GI; 46 (LO RT), Hulton Archive/GI; 47 (UP LE), Heiti Paves/SS; 47 (UP RT), Pictorial Press/AL; 47 (CTR LE), Al Greene Archive/GI; 47 (CTR RT), Ewing Galloway/Bridgeman Images; 47 (LO LE), Scherl/Süddeutsche Zeitung Photo/Granger, NYC—All rights reserved; 47 (LO RT), Paul McErlane/AL

National Geographic supports K–12 educators with ELA Common Core Resources. Visit natgeoed.org/commoncore for more information.

Table of Contents

Who Was Walt Disney?

Have you ever been to Disneyland or Walt Disney World? Maybe you've seen Disney movies. *The Lion King* and *Frozen* are two of the most successful cartoon movies of all time. There are Disney clothes, toys, and books. The Disney name is everywhere, and it all started with one man, Walt Disney.

THE GREATEST ADVENTURE OF ALL IS FINDING OUR PLACE IN THE CIRCLE OF LIFE.

WALT DISNEY PICTURES
presents
THE
LION KING

Over the years, Disney movies have changed from hand-drawn films, such as *The Lion King*, to computer-made ones, such as *Frozen*.

Disney was the creator of Mickey Mouse, one of the best known cartoon characters in the world. For Disney, those Mickey Mouse cartoons were just part of his success.

Disney liked to say that his success began with a mouse. This photo from 1955 shows Disney drawing Mickey.

Disney also created theme parks. Here he points to a drawing of Sleeping Beauty Castle at Disneyland.

Sleeping Beauty Castle being built

Disney was a dreamer from the start, and his dreams kept getting bigger. Some people thought his ideas were too big, or even impossible. But that did not stop Disney. Even though he sometimes failed, he never stopped trying new things.

In His Own Words

"You don't know what you can do unless you try."

He changed the way cartoons were made. He also created a new type of movie. With imagination and hard work, Disney made his dreams come true. He made our world a more fun place to be.

Sleeping Beauty Castle today

Early Years

Walter Elias (ee-LYE-us) Disney was born on December 5, 1901, in Chicago, Illinois, U.S.A. He was the youngest of four boys. His sister, Ruth, was born two years later.

When Disney was four years old, the family moved to Missouri, U.S.A. They settled on a farm near the town of Marceline (mar-suh-LEEN).

Disney in 1902

Disney's parents, Flora and Elias Disney

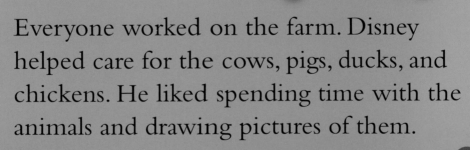

That's a FACT! As a boy, Disney tried to ride on the back of a pig, but he ended up in a mud puddle.

Everyone worked on the farm. Disney helped care for the cows, pigs, ducks, and chickens. He liked spending time with the animals and drawing pictures of them.

Disney had few art supplies, so he sketched on anything he could find—even toilet paper!

His father thought drawing was a waste of time. But Disney's brother Roy encouraged him. Roy was eight years older, but the two boys were close.

As a boy, Disney played and daydreamed under this large cottonwood tree. It's often called the Dreaming Tree. Here he visits it many years later with his brother Roy (left).

A Sticky Problem

One day Disney found a bucket of black, sticky tar. He and Ruth used sticks as paintbrushes to draw on the side of the house. The tar would not wash off. The pictures were still on the house when the family moved a few years later.

When Disney was nine years old, his father sold the farm. Disney cried as he watched the animals being led away by new owners. His lifelong love of animals and nature had begun on that farm.

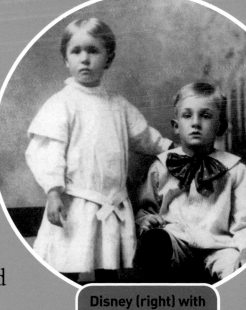

Disney (right) with his sister, Ruth

The family moved to Kansas City, Missouri. Disney's father ran a large newspaper route there. Disney helped deliver papers. He got up at 3:30 a.m. to do his morning paper route before school. After school he delivered the evening paper.

There was little time left for fun, but Disney did not stop drawing. He sketched at school and at night when his homework was done. His father even agreed to let him take an art class on Saturday mornings.

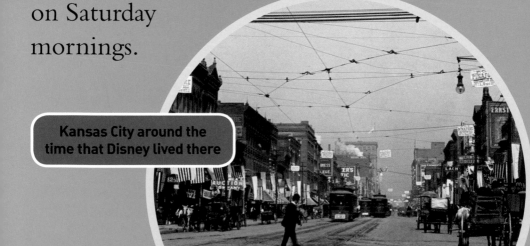

Kansas City around the time that Disney lived there

Disney had a lifelong love of trains.
This train is from the early 1900s.

When Disney was 15, he got a
summer job selling newspapers,
sodas, and snacks to passengers
on trains. Disney liked riding the
trains and seeing new places.

In His Time

When Disney was a boy in the American Midwest in the early 1900s, many things were different from how they are today.

COMMUNICATION: Alexander Graham Bell invented the telephone in 1876, but in 1908 still only 1 in 12 homes had a telephone.

TRANSPORTATION: A few people had cars, but most still traveled by horse and buggy. Long-distance travel was done by train or boat.

ENTERTAINMENT: Going to a theater to see a movie was a new type of entertainment. Films were in black and white and had no sound.

Charlie Chaplin (right) was a famous silent-film star.

MONEY: The average worker earned about $200 to $400 a year. A movie ticket cost 5¢, and Henry Ford's new Model T car sold for $850.

HISTORY: Theodore Roosevelt was president of the United States.

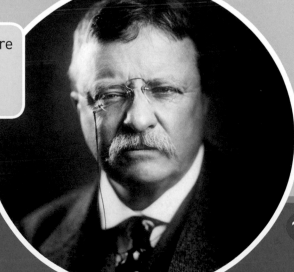

A Young Artist

Soon, Disney's father found work in Chicago, and the family moved again. There, Disney drew cartoons for his high school newspaper. He also took art classes three nights a week.

Over in Europe, World War I was raging. Sixteen-year-old Disney wanted to do his part. He left school and signed up with the Red Cross to drive an ambulance.

Disney was sent to France in November 1918. The war had just ended, but the Red Cross still needed drivers. Disney stayed in France for nine months.

While he was in France, Disney drove an ambulance like these. He drew cartoon figures on the canvas sides.

17

Disney made his Laugh-O-gram cartoons in this building. Today, a group called Thank You Walt Disney is working to restore the building and turn it into an animation museum.

When Disney returned to the United States, he moved back to Kansas City. He got a job with a company that made short films. There, Disney learned about animation.

Two years later, in 1922, Disney left his job and started his own company, called Laugh-O-gram Films. He made short films that took well-known fairy tales and made them funny. Those cartoons were shown in theaters before the main feature.

The Art of Animation

Animation uses a series of pictures to show movement. For example, to show this cat running, an artist made many drawings. In each drawing, the artist made small changes In the positions of the cat's legs. When all those drawings are viewed quickly, one after the other, it looks like the cat is running.

Disney worked hard, but he didn't make enough money to pay all his bills. He had to close the company.

Words to Know

ANIMATION: A way of creating the appearance of movement with a series of pictures

FEATURE: A full-length movie at least one hour long

Back in Business

Disney was 21 years old. He had only $40 in his pocket and no job. He packed everything he owned into one suitcase and took a train to Hollywood, California, U.S.A. The movie business was growing there. He hoped to find work at a movie studio. No one hired him. So Disney started drawing cartoons again.

Word to Know

STUDIO: A place where movies are made or where an artist works

His brother Roy was living in California, too. The brothers teamed up to create a new company, Disney Brothers Studios.

That's a FACT! The name Disney Brothers Studios was later changed to Walt Disney Studios, but Roy continued to be an important part of the company's success.

Roy Disney in 1950

HOLLYWOOD

This is how the famous Hollywood sign appears today. But when Disney arrived in 1923, the sign actually read "Hollywoodland."

Virginia Davis was the first actress to play Alice. She is seen here in a detail from a color poster for one of the Alice Comedies.

Disney worked on a series of short films called the Alice Comedies, which he'd started in Kansas City. They were about a girl who traveled into a cartoon world.

Putting a live person into a cartoon was something new, and people liked it! Disney was asked to make more Alice films. He hired people to keep up with the work.

One of the people Disney hired was
Lillian Bounds. They soon began dating.
On July 13, 1925, they were married.

Disney and his wife,
Lillian, with their dog

New Characters

Disney made 57 Alice films. Then people began to lose interest in them. A man at the company that bought Disney's cartoons and sent them to theaters asked Disney to make a new cartoon. Disney created Oswald the Lucky Rabbit. The Oswald cartoons were a great success.

a poster for an Oswald cartoon

People enjoyed watching cartoons like Disney's before the main feature.

But soon the man who had hired Disney decided he would make the Oswald cartoons himself. Even worse, he hired away almost all of Disney's artists to do the work. Disney lost both the character he had created and most of his best artists. He was angry and sad.

Disney needed a new idea to keep the studio going. He started thinking about a cheerful mouse with big ears. He called the mouse Mortimer (MORE-ti-mur). Lillian Disney didn't like that name. They agreed on another one: Mickey.

It takes 1,440 separate drawings to create one minute of a cartoon.

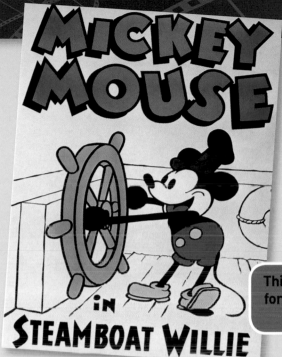

This color poster was made for Steamboat *Willie*'s 50th anniversary in 1978.

As work started on the Mickey Mouse cartoons, something exciting was happening in movies. They now had sound! Disney was determined to add sound to his cartoons.

Steamboat Willie premiered (pree-MEERD) on November 18, 1928. It was Disney's first cartoon with sound. It also introduced Mickey to the world.

Word to Know

PREMIERE:
To be shown for the first time at a theater

a poster for
Flowers and Trees

Disney soon started another series of
cartoons, called Silly Symphonies. One
of them, *Flowers and Trees*, was Disney's first
color cartoon. It was released in 1932. It
was the first animated film to win a special
movie award called an Oscar.

By that time, Disney was so busy creating new ideas that he no longer had time for drawing. He left that to the people who worked for him. He said they did a better job than him anyway.

The Three Little Pigs

Early cartoons were a series of jokes, or gags. With his cartoon *The Three Little Pigs*, Disney worked on telling a story and showing the personalities of his characters. People said that cartoon, released in 1933, was his best so far.

Disney with figurines of characters from *The Three Little Pigs*, as well as Donald Duck and Mickey Mouse

6 COOL FACTS
About Walt Disney

1 Disney's fourth-grade teacher asked everyone in the class to draw a picture of some flowers. Disney's flowers had human faces and arms with hands.

When people visited Disney's home in California, he gave them rides on a small steam-powered train that ran on a half-mile track in his backyard. **2**

3 Disney himself provided the voice for Mickey Mouse until 1946.

4

Disney didn't like being called Mr. Disney. He asked everyone who worked for him to call him Walt.

Disney received an Oscar for *Snow White and the Seven Dwarfs.* Usually, the award is a single gold statue. Disney's award had a regular gold statue plus seven smaller ones.

5

child star Shirley Temple presenting Disney with his special Oscar

6

Disney liked to go to Disneyland early in the morning before it opened. He sometimes drove the fire truck through the park.

Doing the Impossible

In 1933, the Disneys' daughter Diane was born. Three years later, Disney and his wife adopted a baby girl, Sharon. Disney enjoyed spending time with his daughters, but he was also busy at his studio.

Disney was working on his biggest idea yet. He wanted to make a feature-length animated movie. People said his idea was too risky. It would take too much time and money to make an animated feature. And who would go to a theater to watch such a long cartoon? Some made fun of his idea, calling it "Disney's Folly."

Words to Know

RISKY: Involving a chance of something bad happening

FOLLY: A foolish idea

"It's kind of fun to do the impossible."

Disney having fun with his daughters

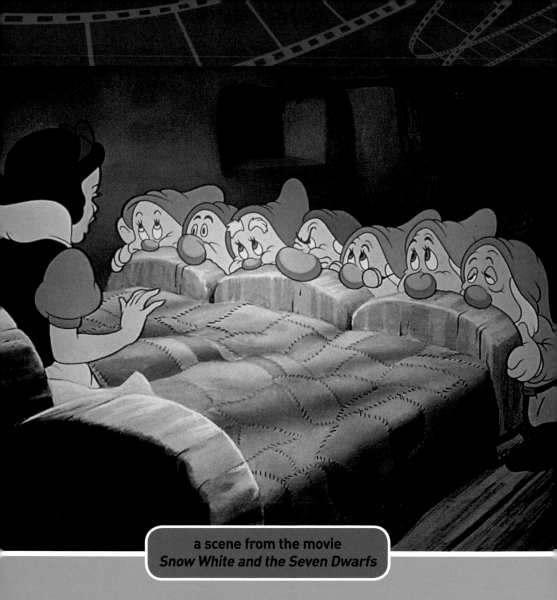

a scene from the movie
Snow White and the Seven Dwarfs

It took three long years to make Disney's animated feature. *Snow White and the Seven Dwarfs* premiered in Los Angeles, California, on December 21, 1937. The movie made people laugh and cry. At the end of the film, they stood and cheered.

The movie made $8 million worldwide, more than any other film up to that time. More animated films followed—*Pinocchio, Fantasia* (fan-TAY-zha), *Bambi,* and *Dumbo.* Walt Disney Studios was a busy place, and Disney was still trying new things.

That's a FACT! Cranky, Blabby, Dizzy, and Burpy were names the Disney team thought about using for the dwarfs.

a poster for *Snow White and the Seven Dwarfs*

a scene from Disney's first live-action movie, *Treasure Island*

Disney started making live-action movies, such as *Treasure Island*. He made nature films, too. Camera crews traveled all around the world to film animals in nature. The first of those films was *Seal Island*, released in 1948.

Word to Know

LIVE-ACTION: Created by filming real people and places

By the 1950s, there was a new type of entertainment—television. In 1954, Disney began his own TV show, *Disneyland*. The program was different each week. The series included cartoons, nature films, and updates on Disney's newest project, a park called Disneyland.

The Mickey Mouse Club

Disney also created *The Mickey Mouse Club*, which first aired on TV in 1955. Every weekday, kids watched the show's stars, called Mouseketeers, sing and dance. The Mouseketeers also introduced cartoons and other short films.

A Happy Place

Disney had been planning his park for years. He wanted it to be a clean, fun place for the whole family. People said it would cost too much. But that didn't stop Disney.

Disneyland opened on July 17, 1955, in Anaheim (AN-uh-hime), California. The day did not go smoothly. People waited in long lines in 100-degree heat. Some rides broke down, and there weren't enough water fountains. Even with first-day problems, Disneyland was a success. One million people visited the park in just the first seven weeks!

In His Own Words

"Disneyland will never be completed. It will continue to grow as long as there is imagination left in the world."

Disney getting ready for opening day at Disneyland

The Dream Lives On

Disney was busy with Disneyland and his television shows. He also worked on a movie based on the book *Mary Poppins*. The movie starred live actors. For fun, Disney added cartoon characters, too. That movie, released in 1964, became one of his most successful films.

a scene from the movie *Mary Poppins*

1901

Born on December 5 in Chicago, Illinois

1920

Begins to learn about animation

1922

Goes into business making Laugh-O-gram cartoons

Mickey Mouse became a mascot of Disney's theme parks, greeting visitors and posing for pictures.

By that time, Disney was buying land for another theme park. It was to be built in Orlando, Florida, U.S.A., and would be even bigger than Disneyland. But Disney did not live to see that dream come true. He died of lung cancer on December 15, 1966.

Word to Know

CANCER: A disease where bad cells grow and spread in the body

1923
Teams up with his brother Roy to create Disney Brothers Studios

1925
Marries Lillian Bounds on July 13

1928
Releases the first Mickey Mouse cartoon, *Steamboat Willie*

Fireworks explode over Cinderella Castle at Walt Disney World.

1932

Releases his first color cartoon, *Flowers and Trees*

1937

Releases his first feature-length animated movie, *Snow White and the Seven Dwarfs*

1954

Introduces *Disneyland*, a television series

Roy completed work on the new park. He named it Walt Disney World. It was his way to honor his brother. The park opened on October 1, 1971.

Today, families enjoy happy times at Disney parks all around the world. Walt Disney Studios continues to be a busy place, releasing new movies each year. Walt Disney never stopped dreaming, and even now his dreams live on.

This statue of Disney and Mickey Mouse greets guests at several Disney parks.

1955
Disneyland theme park opens on July 17

1966
Dies on December 15

1971
Walt Disney World opens on October 1

QUIZ WHIZ

See how many questions you can get right!
Answers are at the bottom of page 45.

Where was Disney born?

A. Marceline
B. Kansas City
C. Chicago
D. Los Angeles

When Disney was _____ years old, he got a job selling snacks and newspapers to passengers on trains.

A. 12
B. 15
C. 16
D. 18

In 1922, Disney started a company that made films he called _____.

A. Silly Symphonies
B. Happy Times
C. Disney Cartoons
D. Laugh-O-grams

4

What was special about *Steamboat Willie*?

A. It was Disney's first film with sound.
B. It was Disney's first film in color.
C. It was Disney's first film with animation.
D. It was Disney's first film with actors.

What was Disney's first feature-length animated movie?

A. *Treasure Island*
B. *Pinocchio*
C. *Snow White and the Seven Dwarfs*
D. *Mary Poppins*

5

6

In 1954, Disney introduced his television show called _____.

A. *Disneyland*
B. *Seal Island*
C. *The Mickey Mouse Club*
D. *Disney's World*

Disney did not live to see the opening of his park Disneyland.

A. true
B. false

7

Glossary

ANIMATION: A way of creating the appearance of movement with a series of pictures

FOLLY: A foolish idea

LIVE-ACTION: Created by filming real people and places

RISKY: Involving a chance of something bad happening

SKETCH: To make a quick drawing showing only the main details

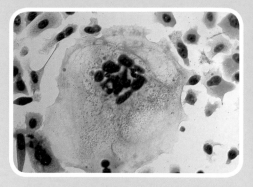

CANCER: A disease where bad cells grow and spread in the body

FEATURE: A full-length movie at least one hour long

PREMIERE: To be shown for the first time at a theater

RELEASE: To send a film to theaters for people to see

STUDIO: A place where movies are made or where an artist works

SYMPHONY: A pleasant variety of sounds, often a long piece of music

Index